Name That Animal!

Whose HOUSE Is This?

Written and Photographed by
Wayne Lynch

Gareth Stevens Publishing
A WORLD ALMANAC EDUCATION GROUP COMPANY

Please visit our web site at: www.garethstevens.com
For a free color catalog describing Gareth Stevens Publishing's
list of high-quality books and multimedia programs, call
1-800-542-2595 (USA) or 1-800-387-3178 (Canada).
Gareth Stevens Publishing's fax: (414) 332-3567.

Library of Congress Cataloging-in-Publication Data

Lynch, Wayne.
    Whose house is this? / written and photographed by Wayne Lynch.
        p. cm. — (Name that animal!)
    Includes bibliographical references and index.
    Summary: Asks the reader to identify various animals from descriptions of
 where they live and provides information about the physical characteristics
 and behavior of each animal.
    ISBN 0-8368-3641-3 (lib. bdg.)
    1. Animals—Habitations—Juvenile literature. (1. Animals—Habitations.)
 I. Title.
 QL756.L96   2003
 591.56'4—dc21   2002036523

This edition first published in 2003 by
Gareth Stevens Publishing
A World Almanac Education Group Company
330 West Olive Street, Suite 100
Milwaukee, Wisconsin 53212 USA

Gareth Stevens series editor: Dorothy L. Gibbs
Gareth Stevens graphic designer: Katherine A. Goedheer

Printed in the United States of America

1 2 3 4 5 6 7 8 9 07 06 05 04 03

Long ago, people lived in dark caves. Later, some people lived in tents made of animal skins or in huts made of grass, sticks, and mud. Today, most people live in houses made of wood, brick, glass, and metal.

Wild animals live in houses that are very different from ours. Some live in rock piles or in clay castles. Others live inside hollow trees. Some dig caves in icy snowdrifts.

Can you name the wild animals that live in the houses pictured in this book?

Early in winter, my mother used her sharp claws to dig a large cave in a snowdrift. Then I was born. I was the size of a tiny squirrel and got cold very easily. To stay warm, I snuggled into my mother's long, white fur. The thick snow of our house also protected me from the chilly winter winds.

Who am I?

4

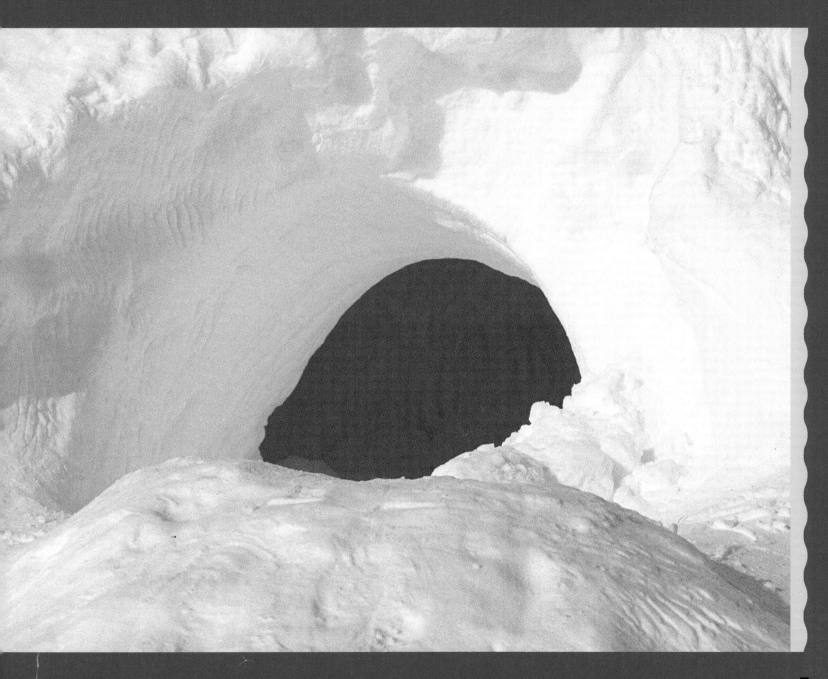

I am a polar bear. I live on the frozen ocean of the Arctic. When I was only four months old, I left my cozy winter den to hunt seals and walruses on the sea ice. The bare skin on the bottoms of my feet is rough, like sandpaper, so I do not slip on the ice.

Beneath its white fur, a polar bear's skin is completely black. Even the inside of its mouth is black.

A hollow tree makes a great house. It protects me from rain and wind and hides me from my enemies. Many animals, including bats, anteaters, lizards, snakes, and even other birds, would like to steal my house. I am able to protect it because I am a large bird, and I have a strong, sharp beak.

Who am I?

I am a macaw. I live in the rain forests of Central and South America. My favorite foods are the nuts of palm trees. I crush their hard shells with my large beak and strong jaws to reach the tasty nuts inside. I use my flexible foot like a hand to hold the nuts while I'm eating them.

Macaws are the largest parrots in the world. Like many parrots, macaws do not sing — they squawk!

Looking at my house of sticks, you probably think I am a beaver. I am not a beaver, but a family of beavers did build my house. Then, after they had cut down all the trees around the pond, the beavers left, and I moved in. I must swim underwater to get inside my new house — but that's easy for me!

Who am I?

I am a river otter. I live in the lakes, rivers, and ponds of North America, often in dens or lodges built by other animals. In muddy water, where I cannot see very well, my long whiskers help me find fish and other foods. I also eat frogs, snakes, and crayfish.

River otters have thick fur coats to keep them warm in cold waters. They also have large webbed feet, so they are very fast swimmers.

I use a house only in summer. To build my house, I dive underwater to get plants, then I pile up the plants to make a soggy floating nest. The deep water around my house keeps me safe from coyotes, foxes, and skunks. Whenever I leave my nest, I cover my eggs with water plants to hide them.

Who am I?

17

I escape from the heat of the Sun and the sharp eyes of hawks and eagles that hunt me by crawling inside termite tunnels. Termites are blind insects about the size of ants. Although they are tiny, they sometimes build castles of clay as tall as houses. The castles are full of secret tunnels where I can hide.

Who am I?

I am a cobra. I live in the tropical forests and on the grasslands of Africa and southern Asia. I hunt, day or night, for mice, birds, rats, frogs, lizards, and even other snakes to eat. The venom in my fangs makes my bite deadly. I am one of the world's most poisonous animals.

When a cobra is frightened, it raises its head high off the ground and flattens its neck to look bigger and scarier.

My house is a burrow. I use my sharp beak and webbed feet to dig the burrow. Sometimes, I put dry grass inside to make my burrow more comfortable. I am surrounded by many neighbors. At the end of each day, I stand outside my house, flap my flippers, and scream like a donkey to let everyone know I am home.

Who am I?

I am a banded penguin. I live along the coast of South America. Unlike many other kinds of penguins, I do not live in a land of ice and snow. In my part of the world, the Sun can be very hot. My burrow protects my eggs and chicks from heat, as well as from rain and wind.

Banded penguins spend their days diving for shrimp, squid, and fish. Because they feed them so much fish, their chicks often become very chubby.

A pile of rocks might not seem like a very good house, but that is where I live. My house is high in the mountains. It is so high that, if you came for a visit, you would have a hard time breathing. At night, the temperature drops below freezing, but I have a coat of thick, woolly fur to keep me warm.

Who am I?

I am a viscacha. I live in South America. Although I look like a rabbit, I am related to woodchucks. Every morning, I like to lie on the rocks in the warm Sun, but I am always watching for hungry eagles, foxes, and mountain lions. When I see danger, I whistle a loud warning.

Without much to eat so high in the mountains, viscachas munch mostly on cactus and dry plants.

Index

More Books to Read

Amazing Journeys: Through a Termite City. Carole Telford and Rod Theodorou (Heinemann Library)

The Magic School Bus Hops Home: A Book about Animal Habitats. Joanna Cole (Scholastic)